The Wright Brothers

History Maker Bios

Ginger Wadsworth

LERNER PUBLICATIONS COMPANY • MINNEAPOLIS

In memory of John Abbott (1927–1966),
United States Navy Captain and pilot on the USS Kitty Hawk

Illustrations by Tim Parlin

Text copyright © 2004 by Ginger Wadsworth
Illustrations copyright © 2004 by Lerner Publications Company

Lerner Publications Company
A division of Lerner Publishing Group
241 First Avenue North
Minneapolis, MN 55401 U.S.A.

Website address: www.lernerbooks.com

Library of Congress Cataloging-in-Publication Data

Wadsworth, Ginger.
    The Wright brothers / by Ginger Wadsworth.
      p.   cm. — (History maker bios)
    Summary: A biography of the two inventors whose 1903 powered, controlled flight of an airplane at Kitty Hawk, North Carolina, made history. Includes bibliographical references and index.
    ISBN: 0–8225–0199–6 (lib. bdg. : alk. paper)
    1. Wright, Orville, 1871–1948—Juvenile literature. 2. Wright, Wilbur, 1867–1912—Juvenile literature. 3. Aeronautics—United States—Biography—Juvenile literature. 4. Inventors—United States—Biography—Juvenile literature. [1. Wright, Orville, 1871–1948. 2. Wright, Wilbur, 1867–1912. 3. Aeronautics—Biography. 4. Inventors.] I. Title. II. Series.
    TL540.W7W24 2004
    629.13'0092'273—dc21
                                            2002154873

Manufactured in the United States of America
1 2 3 4 5 6 – JR – 09 08 07 06 05 04

TABLE OF CONTENTS

INTRODUCTION

It all began on December 17, 1903. Orville and Wilbur Wright, brothers and best friends, were at Kitty Hawk, North Carolina. They were ready to test the Flyer. With Orville at the controls, the Flyer lifted off shakily, under its own motor power, and flew for twelve seconds. Wilbur took his turn next, soaring above the sand dunes.

The Wright Brothers had built and flown the world's first airplane. They changed the way we travel around the world.

This is their story.

1 GROWING UP

Wilbur Wright was born on April 16, 1867. His brother, Orville, was born on August 19, 1871. Wilbur and Orville had two older brothers, Reuchlin and Lorin, and a younger sister, Katharine.

Their mother, Susan Wright, taught her children how to use tools and fix things. They learned to cook and sew, too.

Their father, Milton Wright, was a minister in the United Brethren Church. He kept detailed records about his work and his family. Bishop Wright expected his children to work hard, believe in themselves, and find a purpose in life. Going to school was important. Yet he felt that ten months of school each year was too long. Orv, Will, and Kate were allowed to miss a day or two of school to work on a project. Or they could stay home and read. The house was filled with books.

Oil lamps lit the Wrights' house in Dayton, Ohio. There was a pump for water outside the kitchen door and an outhouse at the rear of the house.

When Orv was seven and Will was eleven, their father gave them a toy helicopter. It was made of wood and paper and powered by a rubber band. Will and Orv wound up the rubber band, and the tiny helicopter skittered into the air.

Orv and Will built new and better helicopter models. Orv even fiddled with one at school. He told his teacher that he was making a flying machine. He might even build one big enough for him to fly in!

Eight-year-old Orv was a prankster who bubbled with ideas.

Will tagged along with Reuchlin and Lorin and their friends. Sometimes Orv and Kate trailed after Will. Will teased Orv when he said words the wrong way. He made Kate cry by making faces at her.

The fields around Dayton were perfect for summer ball games and hide-and-seek. During the winter, Will and his friends played shinny, a kind of ice hockey. Will enjoyed history and geography in school. He was smart and liked living in his own world of ideas.

Will (BACK ROW, CENTER), Lorin (FRONT ROW, RIGHT), and Reuchlin (BACK ROW, 2ND FROM LEFT) were in a club called Ten Dayton Boys.

Orv mostly wanted to tinker—to take things apart and put them back together. He was eager to build kites, after Will showed him how. Orv sold his kites to his friends.

They were teenagers when Susan Wright became ill with tuberculosis. She was weak and needed lots of care. Nineteen-year-old Will stepped in. He took care of his mother for three years, until her death in 1889. Her death was a terrible blow to them all, especially to Will.

Orv had decided to drop out of school and started a printing business. With Will's help, he made a printing press out of a tombstone, buggy parts, and other recycled odds and ends. He published a weekly newsletter, the *West Side News*. Will became the editor. When it failed, the brothers formed Wright & Wright, Job Printers. They printed business cards, posters, flyers, and advertisements for local businesses.

Orv's friend Ed Sines works at the printing business.

In 1892, Orv and Will each bought a bicycle. Will rode out in the country around Dayton. Orv raced other cyclists on a track. Whenever a bicycle broke down, the brothers fixed it. They even repaired their friends' bicycles. Before long, they were known as skilled mechanics.

Bored with the printing business, the brothers wanted to try something new. Will, who was twenty-five, and Orv, age twenty-one, opened a bicycle shop.

THE HISTORY OF THE BICYCLE

The bicycle was invented in the early 1800s. A rider sat between two wooden wheels, pushing the bicycle with his feet. Next came the velocipede, with pedals attached to the large front wheel. The rider might sit as high as five feet off the ground. The safety bicycle, invented in 1885, had chain-driven wheels of equal size and coaster brakes. Cycling became a national craze. By 1886, about a million bicycles were sold in the United States.

2 FROM BICYCLES TO GLIDERS

Wilbur and Orville "lived together, played together, worked together, and in fact, thought together." They even shared a bank account. Working side-by-side in the bicycle shop, they often whistled or hummed the same tune.

Orville wore a large apron over his suit. He didn't want to get dirty. But he loved to take things apart to see how they worked. It was just as much fun to put everything back together.

Dreamy Wilbur ignored the mess on the floor and the smells of glue and oil. Katharine had to remind Wilbur to wash before meals and make sure his clothes were clean.

Wilbur, hard at work in the Wright Cycle shop in 1897

Wilbur and Orville adored Lorin's children, (LEFT TO RIGHT) Milton, Leontine, and Ivonette.

The three of them lived at home with their father. Reuchlin and his family lived in Kansas, but Lorin and his family lived nearby. Orv and Will read stories to their nieces and nephews. They made candy together and put on puppet shows. Orv played his mandolin, and Will played his harmonica. They also loved to play with their nieces' and nephews' toys. "They had a habit of playing with them until they were broken, then repairing them so that they were better than when they were bought," one niece said.

Otto Lilienthal tests his glider. He made almost 2,000 short flights.

Both brothers kept up with the world news. They read about men flying in balloons and ornithopters, machines with flapping wings. Most readers laughed at the stories. But not Wilbur and Orville.

Otto Lilienthal was testing gliders in Germany. Gliders had no motors. They soared with the wind. Lilienthal would race downhill until the glider's wings swept him off the ground.

After many, many successful flights, Lilienthal died in a glider crash in 1896. Wilbur wondered what had gone wrong. Was the glider too heavy? Didn't Lilienthal have enough control over his flight?

Wilbur wrote to the Smithsonian Institution in Washington, D.C. "I believe that simple flight . . . is possible to man. I am an enthusiast but not a crank." He wanted to know more. The Smithsonian sent some information.

Samuel Pierpont Langley, the secretary of the Smithsonian, was testing a flying machine he called an Aerodrome. His remote-controlled model had two pairs of curved wings, a steam engine, and a pair of propellers. It had flown for half a mile until it had run out of steam.

To Fly Like the Birds

From the beginning of time, artists had sketched people and machines with birdlike wings of wood, fabric, or feathers. In 1783, French brothers Joseph and Etienne Montgolfier sent up a painted fabric hot-air balloon over Versailles. The passengers were a sheep, a duck, and a rooster. All three animals returned to earth unharmed.

Wilbur also wrote to Octave Chanute, a retired engineer who had tested gliders on the shores of Lake Michigan. Chanute wrote back to encourage the Wright brothers.

Both brothers watched birds in flight. They agreed that if birds could fly, people should be able to fly in a machine with wings. But they disagreed about how birds controlled their flight. When they disagreed about something, they could argue for hours.

Octave Chanute's glider had wings mounted on rubber springs. That way, the wings could rock back and forth with the wind.

Orville and his friend Ed Sines repair bicycles in the cycle shop.

"'Tis," Wilbur would say, "'Tis not," Orville would argue. In the middle of an argument, they'd often switch sides.

One day in the bicycle shop, Wilbur was twisting a long, narrow, inner tube box. When one end went up, the other went down. All of a sudden, the bent box reminded him of how birds moved their wingtips in the wind. What if he and Orville could figure a way for a pilot to control the bend in the wings of a glider?

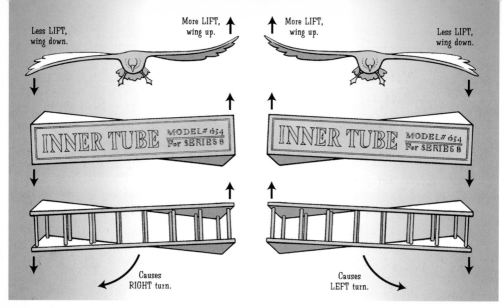

More LIFT, wing up.

More LIFT, wing up.

Less LIFT, wing down.

INNER TUBE MODEL #654 For SERIES 8

INNER TUBE MODEL #654 For SERIES 8

Causes RIGHT turn.

Causes LEFT turn.

The brothers made a glider that could fly like a bird. When one wingtip tilted up, the other tilted down, and the glider turned.

In the bicycle shop, Orville and Wilbur constructed a glider. It was five feet long and was made of wood, wire, and cloth. The wingtips were connected. When the brothers made one wingtip tilt up, the other wingtip would tilt down.

Wilbur picked a windy day to test their model. He flew the glider like a kite. He tossed the glider into the wind like a kite. Using cords running from the wings to sticks he held, the glider climbed and dived on command. It was a huge success!

Wilbur and Orville were eager to build something bigger. It had to be strong enough to hold a person. They also needed a testing place with lots of steady wind and open space.

Wilbur wrote to the U.S. Weather Bureau in Washington, D.C., asking for a list of the windiest weather stations. The brothers picked a place where the wind blew ten to twenty miles per hour. It was a tiny fishing village called Kitty Hawk, on the Outer Banks of North Carolina.

EYES ON THE SKY

Wilbur brought the glider parts to Kitty Hawk in September 1900 by train and boat. At Kitty Hawk, there were miles of soft sand for flying and landing. And there wouldn't be many onlookers to bother them.

Orville followed a few weeks later. The brothers pitched a tent in the sand and finished putting their glider together.

They soon discovered that the Weather Bureau had given them the *average* wind speed. The wind could gust up to sixty miles per hour. They tied their tent to a tree, just to be safe. Orville wrote to Katharine: "When we crawl out of the tent to fix things outside, the sand fairly blinds us. We came down here for wind and sand, and have got them."

The brothers still flew their glider like a kite. They controlled it with handheld lines. After days of testing, they decided it would work with a pilot aboard.

The Wright brothers' tent at Kitty Hawk was buffeted by wind and sand.

Lying face down on the lower wing, Wilbur flies the glider.

Orville, Wilbur, and Bill Tate, the Kitty Hawk postmaster, hauled the glider to the top of a sand dune. Wilbur lay face down on the lower wing. Orville and Bill each grabbed a wingtip and ran into the wind. Wilbur yelled, "Let go!" For a few seconds, the glider rode the breezes above the sand. Wilbur made about a dozen flights that day. In all, he spent two minutes in the air.

By late October, it was time to fold up the tent and go home. The Wright brothers had a bicycle shop to run. But they left with plenty of ideas.

The following year, the brothers brought a new glider to Kitty Hawk. Much to their disappointment, the 1901 glider was hard to fly, even in the strong winds. They wondered if it had something to do with the curve of the wings.

Wilbur (LEFT) and Orville (RIGHT) test the 1901 glider. This model was much more dangerous than the 1900 glider.

Wilbur and Orville went home much earlier than planned. They went right to work. All winter long, they tested wing shapes. The brothers wrote down everything in notebooks. This information helped them put together a new glider. They hoped it would be much better.

TESTING WINGS

To test how wings worked, the Wright brothers built a wind tunnel. The wind tunnel was a box—1½ feet square and 6 feet long—with a fan at one end. They made about two hundred pairs of tiny wings called airfoils. The airfoils were made of metal. They were thin or thick, curved or flat.

The fan blew steady air through the tunnel. Each wing was tested in the tunnel to see how it reacted to moving air. After hundreds of tests, Wilbur and Orville discovered what kind of wing shape would make their glider fly best.

Orville crashes the 1902 glider.

Wilbur and Orville returned to Kitty Hawk in September 1902. For the first time, Orville flew. He warped, or bent, the wingtips to turn left or right. He controlled up and down movements by the forward rudder, or elevator. Then Orville crashed. Luckily, he walked away without a single scrape. But the glider had to be repaired. Orville wondered what had gone wrong.

During one sleepless night, Orville figured out a possible solution. What if the glider's tail could move like a bird's tail?

Orville and Dan Tate launch the 1902 glider. With their changes, "our serious troubles ended," Wilbur said.

He and Wilbur talked it over. They decided to connect wires to the tail and to the wing-warping wires. That way, by shifting his hips, the pilot could twist the wings and turn the tail at the same time.

It worked. When the wind reached about thirty miles an hour, the remodeled glider soared over the sand. "That was the highest wind a gliding machine was ever in, so that we now hold all the records!" Orville wrote.

They had gone over 550 feet. And they had spent twenty-six seconds in the air. Orville and Wilbur had learned how to control flight.

Their 1902 glider flew. But it didn't have an engine. It couldn't take off under its own power, and it would never fly very far. But the brothers were already at work designing an engine. The engine would power propellers that would push the plane into the air. Then they could take off and fly. They wouldn't depend on wind power.

Just before leaving Kitty Hawk, Orv and Will collected shells, sand, and bottles of seawater to bring home to their nieces and nephews.

4 FLYING A POWERED PLANE

When they returned to Kitty Hawk in September 1903, Orville and Wilbur brought the engine they had built. They bolted it to the plane, called the Flyer. With an engine to turn the two propellers, the plane would lift into the air and fly . . . they hoped!

The Flyer was too heavy to lift off with just the wind. It needed the propellers to start it moving before taking off. The brothers put together a long, straight takeoff rail in the sand. Bicycle wheels would guide the aircraft along the rail.

When Orville and Wilbur tested the engine, it rattled and puffed clouds of smoke. The propellers cracked. Then the brothers had problems with the fuel line. Everything took weeks to repair. During another test, a propeller cracked again. Orville hurried home to Dayton to make stronger propellers.

The Wright brothers built a twelve horsepower, gasoline-powered engine to power their Flyer.

By Sunday, December 13, Orville was back. The plane was ready. Even the weather was perfect. But the Wright brothers read and walked on the beach. They had promised their father they would never fly on Sundays.

The winds had died down on Monday. But on the icy cold morning of Thursday, December 17, 1903, they picked up again. It was Orville's turn. The two brothers clasped hands. Then Orville lay on the lower wing.

Standing by the Wright brothers' camp, the Flyer had a forty-foot wingspan and weighed over 700 pounds.

The Flyer took off at 10:35. Winds rocked the plane, and Orville had a hard time controlling it.

The engine clattered and shook. The propellers turned. The aircraft rattled down the track. It lifted off and climbed. It flew!

When the Flyer landed on the sand, the plane had flown under its own power for twelve seconds and gone 120 feet. It was the world's first powered, controlled flight.

Next, Wilbur flew the Flyer for a fifteen-second flight. Orville took another turn. On the fourth flight, Wilbur was in the air for fifty-nine seconds. It was time for the brothers to celebrate.

They telegraphed their father and sister. "Successful four flights Thursday morning. . . . Inform Press home Christmas."

WITNESSING THE FIRST FLIGHT

The brothers raised a small flag above the work shed. It was a signal that a powered flight was about to be attempted. Everyone was invited to watch. Orville and Wilbur wanted witnesses. Five men, two boys, and a dog watched on December 14, 1903, when the Flyer lifted off the ground for only three and a half seconds. Five witnesses showed up on December 17, 1903. After the flight, one man dashed to the post office in Kitty Hawk. "[Darned] if they ain't flew!" he said.

Virginian-Pilot.

VOL. XIX. NO. 68.   NORFOLK, VA. FRIDAY, DECEMBER 18, 1903. TWELVE PAGES.   THREE CENTS PER COPY.

FLYING MACHINE SOARS 3 MILES IN TEETH OF HIGH WIND OVER SAND HILLS AND WAVES AT KITTY HAWK ON CAROLINA COAST

TALLY SHEETS WILL DECIDE CONTEST

U. S. LANDING PARTY FINDS STRONG CAMP OF COLOMBIAN TROOPS

Natives Order American Flag Hauled Down on "Culta 'Bat it Stays That"

TO DEEPEN THE HARBOR AT NORFOLK

Secretary of War to Report to Congress For Making Channel Here 35 Feet Deep for Big Warships

"WANTS CANAL BUILT WITHOUT SUSPICION OF NATIONAL DISHONOR"

Senator Hoar and Gorman in Fiery Debate on Floor of the Senate

NO BALLOON ATTACHED TO AID IT

Three Years of Hard, Secret Work by Two Ohio Brothers Crowned With Success

ACCOMPLISHED WHAT LANGLEY FAILED AT

With Man as Passenger Huge Machine Flew Like Bird Under Perfect Control

BOX KITE PRINCIPLE TWO PROPELLERS

This newspaper reported that the plane had flown three miles. Another called it a "stunt." The real story was not printed in the newspapers.

Back home, the brothers began to build another plane. At Huffman Prairie, northeast of Dayton, the brothers flew first one new and improved Flyer, then the next. Still, there were crashes. Wilbur and Orville kept iodine and bandages handy for scrapes and bruises.

Over the next two years, the brothers built a plane that could fly to the end of a field, turn, come back, and then land safely. On October 5, 1905, Wilbur flew *Flyer III* for over thirty minutes. He covered twenty-four miles before the plane ran out of gas.

Sometimes people came out from Dayton to watch Wilbur and Orville. When newspaper reporters showed up, the weather was often bad or the plane wouldn't fly properly. So Orville and Wilbur never made headlines, except when they did something wrong. Tired of being called names, they decided to show the world what they had truly accomplished.

Soaring above Huffman Prairie, the FLYER III was essentially the world's first practical airplane.

5 FAME

On August 8, 1908, Wilbur flew their new Flyer in France. A huge crowd watched. Newspapers went wild over "the great white bird." France went crazy over Wilbur. Everyone wanted a green racing driver's cap just like Wilbur's.

Wilbur flies the 1908 Flyer over horse-drawn carriages in France.

In September, Orville flew the newest Flyer at Fort Myer, Virginia. After seeing one flight, reporters and army personnel were stunned. Orville Wright was really flying!

Wilbur kept flying in France, breaking record after record. Later, Orville and Katharine joined him. The brothers were famous.

When they returned to Dayton in May 1909, thousands of people greeted them. Marching bands, festivities, and fireworks were part of the day. A carriage and four white horses carried them home. Flags and banners decorated the house.

Shy Will and Orv didn't enjoy all the attention. But it was only the beginning. In the fall of 1909, Wilbur flew along the Hudson River in New York City. More than one million people watched his thirty-three-minute flight.

Dayton, Ohio, welcomes the Wright brothers home with a huge celebration. It included a flag of schoolchildren dressed in red, white, and blue.

The brothers formed the Wright Company on November 22, 1909. Wilbur was president. Orville was vice president. They did not have to repair bicycles anymore. They were rich. Countries were buying their planes and paying them for advice. In February 1912, they bought land overlooking Dayton. Orville and an architect began to design a mansion. It was named Hawthorn Hill.

The house was being built when Wilbur became ill. He had a disease called typhoid fever. He grew sicker and sicker.

Wilbur died on May 30, 1912, at the age of forty-five. Newspapers around the world wrote about Wilbur's death. The family received thousands of sympathy telegrams and a train car full of flowers.

Orville lost interest in work. He played with his nieces and nephews and took them on trips. Orville, Katharine, and their father moved into Hawthorn Hill in 1914.

Later that spring, World War I began in Europe. Orville hoped that planes would be used only to watch for the enemy on the ground. But they were also used to fight. Orville believed that war was terrible.

Orville, Bishop Wright, Katharine, and some of their relatives sit on the lawn at Hawthorn Hill.

With Wilbur gone, Orville's heart wasn't in the airplane business. He sold the Wright Company. Orville was still interested in inventions. He made toys and tinkered in a laboratory he built at Hawthorn Hill.

The war ended in 1918. President Woodrow Wilson appointed Orville to the National Advisory Committee for Aeronautics. The committee looked for ways to improve flight. One of the members was Charles Lindbergh. He and Orville became close friends.

CHARLES LINDBERGH

There were many other heroes in the sky. One was Charles Lindbergh, who in 1927 was the first person to fly solo across the Atlantic Ocean. He flew nonstop from New York to Paris, France. A Wright motor powered his plane, the SPIRIT OF ST. LOUIS. Crowds followed Lindbergh wherever he went, even when he stopped in Dayton, Ohio, to visit his friend Orville Wright.

Orville still loved tinkering. He built a clothes-rinsing machine, a toaster, and a stove. He was tinkering with a doorbell on January 27, 1948, when he had a heart attack. He died three days later at the age of seventy-six.

Orville and Wilbur had shared the same dreams. Their airplane changed the world. Yet Orville had said, "I got more thrill out of flying before I had ever been in the air at all—while lying in bed thinking how exciting it would be to fly."

TIMELINE

WILBUR WAS BORN ON APRIL 16, 1867.
ORVILLE WAS BORN ON AUGUST 19, 1871.

In the year . . .

1893   the Wright brothers opened a bicycle shop.

1899   Wilbur discovered wing-warping.   Age 32
the Wright brothers built and flew a glider.

1900   they tested their 1900 glider at Kitty Hawk, North Carolina, in September and October.

1901   they tested their 1901 glider at Kitty Hawk in July and August.

1902   they tested their 1902 glider at Kitty Hawk in September and October.
they began to build a motor for their glider.

1903   Orville made the world's first powered   Age 32
flight on December 17 at Kitty Hawk, North Carolina.

1905   the Wright brothers built the *Flyer III.*

1908   Wilbur flew the *Type A Flyer* in France
Orville flew the *Type A Flyer* for the Army Signal Corps in Virginia.

1912   Wilbur Wright died on May 30.   Age 45

1917   The United States entered World War I.

1918   World War I ended.

1920   Orville was appointed a member of the National Advisory Committee for Aeronautics.

1932   the Wright Memorial was dedicated at Kitty Hawk, North Carolina.

1938   the Wright brothers' bicycle shop and family home were moved to historic Greenfield Village, Michigan.

1948   Orville died on January 30.
the 1903 Wright Flyer was installed at the   Age 76
Smithsonian Institution on December 17.

CONTROLLED FLIGHT

Inventors like Otto Lilienthal and Octave Chanute had figured out how to make wings that flew. Other inventors worked on engines to power flying machines. But only the Wright brothers realized that a pilot would need to control a flying machine in all three axes. These axes are pitch, roll, and yaw.

Pitch is the up and down movement of a plane's nose.

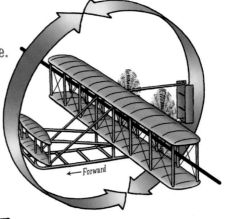

Roll is the side-to-side movement of a plane.

Yaw is the side-to-side movement of a plane's nose.

FURTHER READING

Berliner, Don. *Before the Wright Brothers.* Minneapolis: Lerner Publications, 1990. The stories of attempts at flight before 1903. Includes Lilienthal, Chanute, and Langley.

Bingham, Caroline. *Big Book of Airplanes.* New York: Dorling Kindersley, 2001. Facts and photos of airplanes, from barnstormers to passenger jets.

Provenson, Alice and Martin. *The Glorious Flight: Across the Channel with Louis Bleriot.* New York: Viking, 1983. The story of Louis's quest for a plane that he could fly across the English Channel and that first flight. Winner of the Caldecott Award.

Schulz, Walter A. *Will and Orv.* Minneapolis: Carolrhoda Books, 1991. A fictionalized history of the first flight through the eyes of a boy.

Wallner, Alexandra. *The First Air Voyage in the United States: The Story of Jean-Pierre Blanchard.* New York: Holiday House, 1996. A story about the first balloon flight in the United States, made by a Frenchman and his dog in 1793.

WEBSITES

Wright Brothers Aeroplane Company and Museum of Pioneer Aviation
An amazing cyber-museum of the Wright brothers' life work. Includes many interactive features.

The Wright Brothers—Henry Ford Museum and Greenfield Village
<www.hfmgv.org/exhibits/wright/default.asp>
A tour of the historical village where the Wright brothers' home and bicycle shop now reside.

Wright Brothers National Memorial
<www.outerbanks.com/wrightbrothers/> A site showing the National Park Service memorial in North Carolina.

SELECT BIBLIOGRAPHY

Crouch, Tom. *The Bishop's Boys: A Life of Wilbur and Orville Wright.* New York: W. W. Norton, 1989.

Crouch, Tom. "On Wheels and Wings." In *Inventors and Discoverers,* edited by Elizabeth Newhouse. Washington, D.C.: The National Geographic Society, 1988.

Culick, Fred E. C., and Spencer Dunmore. *On Great White Wings: The Wright Brothers and the Race for Flight.* New York: Hyperion, 2001.

Freedman, Russell. *The Wright Brothers: How They Invented the Airplane.* New York: Holiday House, 1991.

Howard, Fred. *Wilbur and Orville: A Biography of the Wright Brothers.* New York: Alfred A. Knopf, 1987.

INDEX

Acknowledgments

For photographs and artwork: © Bettmann/CORBIS, pp. 4, 24, 35, 39, 40, 43; Library of Congress, pp. 7, 10, 11, 14, 15, 19, 23, 25, 31, 32, 33, 36, 38, 41; From the Collections of Henry Ford Museum and Greenfield Village, pp. 8, 9; © Hulton-Deutsch Collection/CORBIS, pp. 16, 27; American Heritage Center, University of Wyoming, p. 18; Laura Westlund, p. 20; © CORBIS, p. 28.

Front cover (both), Travel Information Division, Department of Conservation and Development, Raleigh, NC. **Back cover**, © Bettmann/CORBIS.

For quoted material: pp. 13, 23, Marvin K. McFarland, editor, *The Papers of Wilbur and Orville Wright* (New York: McGraw-Hill, 1953, 2001); pp. 15, 19, Ivonette Wright Miller, compiler, *Wright Reminiscences* (Dayton, OH: Privately printed, 1978); pp. 17, 34 (sidebar), Fred E. C. Culick and Spencer Dunmore, *On Great White Wings: The Wright Brothers and the Race for Flight* (New York: Hyperion, 2001); pp. 24, 28, Russell Freedman, *The Wright Brothers: How They Invented the Airplane* (New York: Holiday House, 1991); p. 34, telegram to Bishop Wright from Orville Wright, December 17, 1903; p. 37, Tom D. Crouch, *The Bishop's Boys: A Life of Wilbur and Orville Wright* (New York: W. W. Norton & Company, 1989); p. 43, Orville Wright, *How We Invented the Airplane: An Illustrated History*. edited by Fred C. Kelly (New York: Dover Publications, 1983).